THE WAY TO WHEN

THE WAY TO WHEN

The Poetry of Jeff Bresee

JEFF BRESEE

LitPrime
"Your story is our priority"

LitPrime Solutions
21250 Hawthorne Blvd
Suite 500, Torrance, CA 90503
www.litprime.com
Phone: 1-800-981-9893

Published by LitPrime Solutions   08/21/2023

ISBN: 979-8-88703-283-2(sc)
ISBN: 979-8-88703-284-9(e)

Library of Congress Control Number: 2023913455

CONTENTS

THE WAY TO WHEN

A million ways to spend a day,
not tried them all but have to say
that if I had the way to when,
I'd quiet find and open then
the pages of the poet's hand,
then fly away to distant land.
Or feel the fire of deep desire,
submersed in words, I'd never tire.

I'd float through worlds that few have known,
no boundaries there, no thoughts of home.
Not caring what is real or dream
as feelings flow like crystal streams.

Which feelings I am lost to find
inside my heart, inside my mind.
In daily walk amongst the dead,
cast to the sea with boots of lead.

I feel that I would drown and die,
my only hope the thought that I
can find again the way to when
I'm all alone with such a friend -
the healing words of poet's hand…
the only words I understand.

JEZEBEL

Dim lit, damp, and distant corner,
torn from dream of vapor's fold.
Slow descent to worlds divided,
nothing hot and nothing cold.

Long ago this soul forgotten,
cast off in the ides of youth.
Un-forgiven deeds left hiding
beneath the stone of burden's proof.

Wait to see if fate redeems her.
Wait to hear if time repeals.
Sentence passed down just to mar her.
Word and deed like flint and steel.

'Jezebel!' they mock to call her,
waging war against the skin.
Pressed on by the mob's directive,
let the judgment now begin.

Scrutinize each blood-stained footprint,
left across the ice drawn field.
Hide the ones who hold her province.
Never bend. No, never yield.

For from that damp and distant corner
ever flows the world of hate,
through the veins of those who think they...
hold the key to Heaven's gate.

BETWEEN MIND AND EYES

How vast is the reach of the universe wide?
How great be the distance between mind and eyes?
How far in both ways does the length of time go?
What distance exists between God and each soul?

Illusive the answer to each of these be.
Perspective controls how we think, what we see,
how we judge and interpret the concepts at hand,
the things we consider and just where we stand.

We all live in bubbles of what we believe.
We think we see what everybody else sees,
but that which we see at the end of the day
is through a glass, darkly, yeah just like they say.
And someday we're all in for quite a surprise…
when we learn the distance between mind and eyes.

ONE HAIR

I thought to change one hair tonight
from white to black, atop my head.
It seemed a try would be alright
while lying here upon my bed.

I called out to the powers that be
in all their forms amidst the sky,
but nothing changed at all for me
though I had given my best try.

I guess it's human nature
to control the things at hand.
To try and make sure everything
works out the way you planned.

We swear upon by the heavens
and it brings down all the rain.
We swear upon the earth and find
it only leads to pain.

We swear upon our heads and find out
just how much we lack,
for we cannot so much as make…
one white hair turn to black.

…Ref Matthew 5:33-36

YET AGAIN

The feeling
haunts me
time and time again.
I feel it as it's coming
like a scent upon the wind.

Like wind across the predator
wafts out to warn the prey.
So likewise, all I know and feel
screams - "Turn and run away!"

But something deep inside me
in a way I can't explain,
finds pleasure in the desecration,
need inside the pain.

So, mind and heart and faculty
drink of the traitor's blood,
and render my will helpless
like a reed against the flood.

Then yet again I falter,
for I now become as they.
The predator has full control...
I want to be the prey.

AT THE DOOR

Curled up in the corner
in dead of the night.
Afraid of darkness
and praying for light.

Eyes peer from the ceiling.
Hands reach from the floor.
Hearts beat from the walls
and he stands at the door.

No chemical shields me.
No masquerade hides.
The sweat of my body,
the fear in my eyes.

He's pounding and pounding
and growing in strength.
He's growing in hunger,
and looking for prey.

He whispers to call me
from deep in my mind.
With lies and with luring
each weakness he finds.

But I know what he wants
yes, I know where it leads.
I've scars to remind me
of all the past deeds.

But the door he can't open
and that's why he calls.
So, I'm curled in the corner…
afraid that I'll fall.

FOR THE ONE

Love is a game, a journey of sorts,
a search for the one who is right.

And of all the seekers, just what do they know,
are not all just travelers at night?

For it seems in darkness they search hill and dale,
hoping to find their true love.

Awash in the masses, a literal throng,
mixed in amongst push and shove.

And so, as you seek for to find it you must,
consider what true love's about.

It's not about finding who you can live with…
but who you cannot live without.

PURPOSE & DESIRE

Nothing can stop the unquenchable fire,
fed by the flame of the deepest desire.

Born of a purpose, intent that is true
in the one who's determined to do what they do.

The one who believes it can always be done.
The one who won't quit till the battle is won.

The one who gets up every time that they fall.
The one who dreams big, regardless how small

they may seem in this world of confusion and doubt.
No, nothing can stop one who's figured it out –

that the universe bends to the purpose and fire
of the one who holds true… to their deepest desire.

LATE AUTUMN

It's a feeling that has no words to describe,
when the late autumn leaves fade color.
Quietly waving a final goodbye
in the chill as morning mist hovers.

It's something between a pure feeling of peace
and a loneliness down to the bone.
Perfect tranquility rests on the air,
but the sadness won't leave you alone.

Life has a way of drifting in waves,
up and down through the moments we live.
Yet lurking below in the dim and the cold
are so many things buried that give

hidden purpose to cry. Is there some reason why
we go on always holding it in?
We should learn from the trees who let go, so in Spring...
they can always start over again.

INTO PILES

What in the world are we doing?
Who are we trying to beat?
It seems like we live our lives running,
as if we are losing our seats.

We never stop building up towers.
We never stop spinning around.
We never stop piling up into piles
everything that we've torn down.

Is it that we are pursuing
happiness, like the old phrase?
Or are we chasing the concept of such
blindly straight into the grave?

Somebody please in all honesty
look me right square in the eyes,
and tell me the lifestyle we base it all on
won't ultimately lead to demise.

It's happened throughout all of history,
each nation eventually falls.
So, history repeats and we all lose our seats...
chasing happiness into the wall.

CRUCIFIXION

They say that the truth is a hard thing to take,
but maybe it's time that we see -
that we as a people are nothing but fake,
ensuring that's how it will be.

We stand up demanding there's tolerance,
doing so with our fists in the air.
It's truly the oddest dance ever been danced,
hypocrisy beyond compare.

We claim we want peace, but we seek the next fight
as we keep our guns close to the door.
Convincing ourselves that we stand for what's right
when the truth is we're actually just bored.

We say that we want to be free men,
while we ride our past into the ground.
We claim that we run from our demons,
but we really just keep them around.

And we live our lives waiting for the next offense,
needing others to kindle the flame.
We're a common collective without common sense
like the scarecrow not having a brain.

So, let's go on pretending we live for the truth,
but the truth is we're living a lie.
For each soul who actually lives for the truth…
we find a way to crucify.

BEAUTY

I see it time and time again
that beauty's made by what is spent.

A beauty that demands a price,
with outer glow and inner ice.

And observation seems to tell
it's only as deep as the well.

For come the day the well runs dry…
such beauty simply waves goodbye.

MERCY

The stars that fill the midnight sky
or single grains of sand,
cannot compare to all his works
too vast to understand.

What number counts the drops of rain
that make the oceans wide?
How many hours and days and years
fill up eternal life?

How far the furthest star lies from
the meager grasp of man?
How far across this universe
hath he stretched forth his hand?

What mercy fills The Father's heart
which grants us time to grow?
Too much for us to comprehend...
Too much for us to know.

I F

If I woke up and worked every day
with a calm resolute execution of plans,
or perhaps at least stayed on approximate track
with the basic things for which I stand.

If with a small grain of faith I'd hold the course,
knowing that by small things come the grand.
Then I think I'd be dangerous, I'd finally be…
an instrument in the Lord's hands.

NEW DAY

Have you ever come to the end of the day,
and can run the clock back play by play,
and can add it up that supposedly
it was the day it was suppose to be,
but somehow it seems that no time has gone
like a broken record playing on and on,
and you think back through all the things you've done -
every day every deed bleeding into one,
and you can't help but feel just a little fear
and hopelessness, cuz it isn't clear
what it's all about, why you rise each day,
fight the fights you fight, play the games you play,
do the things you do, "Just what the hell for",
for you've done it all a thousand times before,
and could keep on going til the bitter end,
and perhaps you will but what purpose then
does it serve, and so your left with not
but to sigh and deal with what you've got,
and just keep moving for you know what they say…

tomorrow will be a brand-new day.

RESOLUTION

What happens when you finally decide
to change what you're doing and swallow your pride?
Is it like when the fog clears away
and you find where you stand?

Or is it more like the unveiling of art,
struck by what you see yet unsure in your heart,
because it is nothing at all
like what you had planned?

For with resolution comes new eyes to see,
and new understanding of how things can be.
Yes, new faith that changes the path
of what lies ahead.

For everything's different the day you decide
to follow your heart and let go of your pride.
You're no longer a prisoner...
but rather a free man instead.

ILLUSIONS

Pretend not to notice.
Pretend you don't see.
Protect at all cost
your illusions of me.

Don't read what I write
on the lines of my page,
you'll only find flaws
that you've long wished away.

Just keep smiling at me,
I'll keep smiling at you.
You be who you are
and I'll do what I do.

I'll try not to let
all the things in my mind
stray far from my pages,
or too out of line.

But I can't promise much
for my pen won't allow
the truth to be hidden,
so I don't know how

I can be who I am,
yet the one who you see.
So, protect at all cost
your illusions of me.

And don't read what I write,
it's far easier then
to see me through my smile…
instead of my pen.

AT THE LEDGE

Each time before when I had fallen, landing in the pit below,
I found upon the ground were words that I could gather up to build,
a latticework of scaffolding to climb upon so I could go
back to the surface with the crowd, but every time I found that still

I'd stay close to the ledge not knowing why I didn't walk away.
I told myself it wasn't wise. I asked, "why don't you ever learn?"
It seemed t'was in my blood forever, an unexplained desire to stay,
a search for reasons I could finally give up once again and turn

to take that foolish step and plunge myself back in the pit of pain
where I would sip it down as liquor, custom stilled to quench the thirst.
It had become the only way I knew to feel something again,
a custom-made handcrafted sculpture of what was to me the worst.

But somewhere in that dreaded cycle, midst the chore of gathering words,
I found some until then passed over. No, t'was not at all by chance.
I knew they were those long ago while in my youth I'd onetime heard,
but I had never chose to use them, they seemed foolish at a glance.

They were to me the words of fable, used to herd the crowd above,
but in my hour of desperation there was nothing else to do
and so, I started sifting through them til I found the word of "love"
which left me standing, staring at it til I'd fully thought it through.

This was the word I had avoided. I felt it was so overused.
It seemed to mingle every single poem and book and tale and song,
but in that moment standing there I realized I'd been confused,
that everything I had associated it with had been wrong.

For in the pile I'd found it in were other words I'd also passed
over and I must admit, I done so all the while in fear.
Won't ever understand it but, I finally opened up and asked
God to help me, then I stood in silence wondering if he'd hear.

But I was soon distracted for I watched these words, before my eyes,
move out from the pile where one by one they all aligned themselves
into the most poetic prose, which as I read it made me cry
and when I wiped the tears away, I looked around and found myself

atop a mountain, high above the land below, no longer near
the pit of pain. I stood there for a long time taking in the view,
and as I did the message that the words formed became very clear.
The word of "love" stood boldly in my mind and I knew what to do.

The years have now passed on ere since that time I finally changed
my ways.
Would like to say I've never since come close unto the pit of pain
but I admit, I still go there to celebrate my darkest days,
and when I'm there I stand close to the edge to look back down again.

But now each time I stand there, I no longer feel the way I did.
I'm not there to fall, but rather simply view it from the ledge above.
I guess I like the feeling I get when I walk away instead,
knowing that it's possible… because I finally learned of love.

BROKEN HALOS

Heard a song of broken halos,
folded wings that used to fly.
Wondered why I go where I go.
Yeah, broken halos as miles went by.

Angels used to come and teach me,
now they've gone another way.
Don't blame them, I told them they should
find another soul to save.

Stared at the darkness and let my mind go,
it took me places I used to shine.
The song kept playing – broken halos.
Yeah, broken halos and this one's mine.

Don't go looking for a reason.
Don't go asking Jesus why.
Some folded wings don't have a reason.
Somehow, they lost the will to fly.

I've seen my share of broken halos,
tried to mend some. I've tried to give.
I never thought someday I'd join them.
I guess it happens in the lives we live.

I drove in silence for long time,
thought of the angels in the grand sublime.
Wondered if they'd ever fallen…
Broken halos that used to shine.
Yeah, broken halos and this one's mine.

Song: Chris Stapleton – Broken Halos

JOT & TITTLE

I had to trade another jot,
I had to sell a tittle.
I had to cuz they told me that
I had to give a little.

I had to sit and wonder at
the setting of the sun,
what giving just a little costs…
when all is said and done.

THE QUESTION

Depression and heartache and yearning -
common throughout all the years,
general amongst all the masses,
driven by so many fears.

It's truly the struggle of ages,
despite born of mansion or cave.
Is life the thing that you're living,
or is it life that you crave?

It's tied to a question so simple -
just what do you live your life for?
Do you live to live in the moment,
or are you searching for more?

But also, it boils down to choices,
just how you spend your free time.
And of opportunity, what do you take -
do you grab and try to align
the way that you're living with all that you want?

That's really the question you see.
The one that you'll spend your days looking back on…
throughout all eternity.

CATCH 22

When forever finally comes to town, not sure I want to be around
when it stands outside to knock upon my door.
I'll hide inside, not make a sound, turn out the lights,
get on the ground, lay in the darkest shadow of the floor.

And if forever's not deterred, no worry I'll plan for the worst.
I'll wait it out, I'll stock up every shelf.
I'll let forever knock all day and hope it finally goes away,
"don't answer" is what I'll sit and tell myself.

And if forever starts to pound hard on the door to knock it down,
I'll stack the furniture up high and deep.
I'll nail some boards, I'll brace, I'll wedge.
I'll cross my heart and make a pledge that –
"While forever's there I'll never sleep!"

For in the end, I know I'll win.
I'll never let forever in, nor ever let it have its' way with me.
And I'll not step outside again. Yes, can't you see I'm bound to win.
Forever locked inside… is where I'll be.

STRANGERS UNAWARE

How odd this ragged stranger seems
who jarred me from my frozen stare,
at dust and dreams and other things
for which I spend my time and care.

No other man hath paid him mind,
no nod, nor smile, nor kindness shown.
No, none at all hath lent him time.
No good man opened up his home.

So, what is lost if I like they
wave off a hand and turn back in,
and quickly block the guilt away
that comes from having been like them?

For not but dread his presence seems.
His very sight a cause to stare,
at rags and seams and other things,
for which he has no means to care.

Thus, I suppose I'll lend a dime.
"Oh, what the hell! Here take it all."
How little it be in the end…
when from our eyes the scales do fall.

INSIDE

Seasons change as years go by,
winter's cold and summer's dry.

Life is hard in many ways,
yet rings are formed as seasons change.

So, although not but bark we see...
inside there is a true beauty.

FAILURE

I tried today and failed again.
I've tried so long I don't know when
it ever went the way of which I planned.

I've given up on wondering why.
I've learned it doesn't help to cry,
nor does it pay to try and understand.

But each time that I stumbling fall,
I rise with my back against the wall
resolved to bury disappointment's ire.

"Get up, keep going everyday!"
"Don't ever let it have its way!"
That's what I tell myself to feed the fire.

That burns deep down inside my heart
and urges, "Make another start!"
"Don't worry that you've
failed each time before."

"For if you always rise again,
you cannot fail, so surely then
the day will come...
and you'll have your reward."

TIIL TIME STANDS STILL

It was a beautiful story,
I wish it was my own.
It makes me think of you
so, every now and then
I turn it on.

Was the first song we danced to,
it made us fall in love.
Now every time it plays
I see your face,
you're all I think of.

Why does it seem true loves
are always kept apart?
Is it cruel fate,
a form of bait
that's used to crush the heart?

Or is God to blame
for all this pain,
or maybe we're just blind.
Well, I don't really know...
I'm just missing you tonight.

But I still see you in my dreams,
and I still hold you up in my arms.
Each time the little things bring
you back in my mind,
I find you're still inside my heart.

So, I don't care how long time goes on,
I'll sit and wait til time stands still.
Where nothing ever can keep us apart again.
If I have to wait until forever…
then I will.

DAYS END

The days don't seem to give a damn,
they march in step of time.
They stare ahead with eyes of steel
while never breaking line.

They torture me with disregard,
they tread upon my soul.
They seem so unaware I'm here,
they simply come and go.

I once believed the day would come,
I hoped that it would give
the thing that I was searching for -
a reason I should live.

But in the end my hope was vain
cause nothing's ever come.
I'm tired of holding on and so
I feel the fight is done.

And so, I sit as night rolls in,
the choice is mine to make.
The glare across the steel call out,
"What action will you take?"

EXIT

It's finally the day to come,
blood mixing in.
Flows like a river
through oceans of sin.

Long past the point
where the numbness was new.
Long past believing
that anything's true.

Steel against flint,
only flash in this night.
Desperate to see
but it only ignites,

the gasoline soaked
twisted rags in my soul.
No way to stop it
and nowhere to go.

You can only get up
til the falls break your bones.
Can only lose so much
before you're alone.

You can only give so much
and once it's all gone…
you paint on a smile
and pretend to go on.

NO REGRET

You can buy land and home across this world made of stone,
gathering more into barns than the rest.

You can travel and see every sight there may be
under Heaven from East to the West.

You can spend every day finding more ways to pay,
grabbing all you can possibly get.

But remember there's something worth far more than these…
to die without any regret.

THINGS

Things to adorn yourself.
Things for your home.
Things of a thousand kind,
what do you own?

Gather it all til you have everything,
but know this that when the day's done –

despite all your things
you don't have a damn thing…
if the sun sets and you've got no one.

TIMELESS CHILL

Granite grandeur draped in snow,
soft whisper falls, clear water flows.

No hand extends to measure time,
no cares ascend, no worries find.

For purpose fades into the still,
a tranquil peace here in the chill.

What part of time and space am I?
So small beneath the endless sky.

A speck of dust, a grain of sand...
yet cradled in the Master's hand.

IN THE MIDDLE

In the middle of life there's a moment of still.
Reminiscing, regretting, "Is there point in it all?"
Looking out in both ways from the top of the hill
as I tumble and shrink to an infinite small.

For I know forever has no end of days,
it leaves me to contemplate just who I am?
And I know that size never ends in both ways,
when you sit in infinity, is there a plan
where we have significance? Any at all?
It seems we are not but a quark in the sea,
yet at the same time I can't help but recall
a simple concept that was once taught to me –

that we are God's children, of infinite worth.
The thought of such gives me that moment of still,
where it becomes clear why I am here on the Earth.
In the middle of life… from the top of the hill.

COME WINTER

When will it be that it's my time to go?
I see all the signs in the air.
Must I wait through storms til there's nothing but snow,
or is there a milder path there?

When I was young, I never spent time
nor took any thought just to sit by and think.
I guess there was no need when weather was fine,
but seasons have passed in a blink.

But somehow there's comfort here watching leaves fall,
though they be the last on the tree.
For I had the chance to experience it all...
may winter's snow soon set me free.

THAT DAY IN JUNE

I sat today midst the happy smiles
of a children's song, and for just a while
I was happy too, for what else should come
from a happy day and a happy song.

But, it came again just like every June,
when I feel the pain of an open wound
that on every other day I keep
hidden far from view, buried oh so deep.

But I guess that's why they made the day,
so that folks like me can't just walk away
from the hidden chambers, vaults and tombs
where ghosts like this are left to loom.

Waiting for the chance to emerge again,
on that day in June, on the one day when
I can only sit choking back the tears…
while the children sing and the ghosts appear.

FALLING APART

Sometimes it doesn't go the way
you thought it would at all.

Sometimes the pieces all line up
though randomly they fall.

Sometimes I guess you're better off
just following your heart.

Cuz sometimes it can still work out…
though you're falling apart.

THE REASON

This is the reason I do what I do.
A rhyme, a song in shades of blue.
Connections made to a million ties.
The longing stare of a million eyes.

Peering out from the darkness, soul by soul.
Bound by the sound of every note.
Bound by the beat of the rhythmic drum.
Bound by the voice of the chosen one.

Chosen to carry the weight of them all.
Chosen to suffer, chosen to fall.
Chosen to feel what they've placed on the shelf,
feelings they no longer feel for themselves.

Feelings that haunt like a cry in the night.
Feelings that keep me from feeling alright.
Feelings that come from the one all alone,
the one beaten down, the one far from home.

The one long neglected, the one who must hide,
the one who can't share what their holding inside.
The one who is broken, the one who's been marred,
the one been abused with the deepest of scars.

The one who has fallen down time after time.
The who has come to the end of the line.
They're searching and yearning and hoping I'll give -
a reason to go on. A reason to live.

So then ask me. I'll tell you, the reason I'm blue…
is because of the reason I do what I do.

TORN

Sometimes love is easy, so natural and pure,
but often it isn't that clear.
Like fog in the morning makes traveling unsure,
not knowing which way you should steer.

For what comes the day you must make the hard choice,
between two you desperately you need?
It's like choosing whether to hear or have voice,
no matter the answer you bleed.

Then how do you make a decision like this,
when there's not one right thing to do?
You choose and you lose and you try to go on…
as you live with a heart torn in two.

LOVE ENOUGH

Love has so many forms by which it shows itself each day,
in simple acts of kindness made in quite heartfelt ways.

Sometimes it takes a hand and spends the time to show it cares.
Sometimes it takes a few steps back while broken hearts repair.

And every time two lovers finally cross each other's path,
it jumps with joy to have the chance to work its favorite task.

But love's diversity is not just shown by different means.
There's also different depths in just how pure true love can be.

And in its purest form love does not ask how tight we hold,
but rather that we love enough… to let the other go.

FREEFALL

Sat through another non-eventful free fall through the ceiling
while trying hard to feel something despite the way I'm feeling.

Trying hard to find my way back to the time of when,
I didn't have to sit in this damn chair time and again.

For every day now seems a bit more like the day before.
Just like a cross between a treadmill and revolving door,

where weeks and months and years all seem to be as one long day.
And I sit waiting, hoping that the numbness goes away.

That perhaps someday I will finally learn to feel again,
where I can feel connected to a loved one or a friend,

or maybe feel excited at some simple little thing,
or cry, or laugh, or things like that instead of suffering.

For all I do now days is sit, as if the clock stood still,
watching everyone around and wishing I could feel

the things that they all seem to feel so very naturally.
And I sit hoping, wondering… if that ever can be me.

LIES WITHIN

I'd take a knife and cut it out
like some deep-down infected gout
if only it were there under my skin.

I'd prick a vein and let it bleed,
free flowing, nothing to impede
if I thought it were streaming deep within.

I'd amputate it bit by bit
til there was nothing left of it,
then throw it piece by piece into the grind.

I'd heat a rod to glowing red,
then press and cauterize instead
of letting it live on, but I can't find

just where it is inside in me.
I've stared into my eyes to see,
but all the mirror shows are signs of age.

I've knelt and prayed and tried to hold.
I've walked the line while growing old
but somehow, I can never turn the page.

And so, I guess all I can do -
keep going. I suppose it's true,
you cannot just give up and let it win.

So, I will hide the way I feel,
and try to find a way to deal...
with the hidden pain that lies within.

THESE THINGS THAT I PRIZE

Most people have a lot,
most have a list
of gidgets and gadgets
and trinkets to buy.

It's just human nature,
there's no harm in this,
but lately
I'm wondering why.

For as I've grown older,
I have realized
(I've had to,
for it is a matter of fact)

while caring for all of
these things that I prize,
everything I own...
owns me right back.

LABOR IN THE FIELD

Some were hired at the break of day, a price to work the field.
Then others hired each passing hour and given the same deal.

And when the eve was drawing nigh the Master with good will
looked out and saw some in the streets who yet were waiting still.

So, then he went to them and asked, "Why have ye labored not?"
They answered, "We have not been hired though labor we have
sought."

And so, the Master stretched his hand and offered them the deal,
which gladly they accepted and they moved into the field.

But when the ones who'd worked all day came forth to claim their pay,
they were offended when the saw all had received the same.

And they began to murmur much, "Does not the Master care
that we have labored more than they? This simply isn't fair!"

But then Master stood and said, "Good friend I've done no wrong.
Have not I paid as we agreed? Is not my word yet strong?"

And then he asked the ones who felt their payment was unfair,
"Is thine eye evil because I'm good?" And silence filled the air.

For they did not appreciate the good things they'd received.
The value of the wage alone was all that they could see.

They'd missed the point of why they worked.
They never gained the yield...
the true joy that comes to the souls who labor in the field.

Ref: Matthew 20: 1-15

TIME WANES THIN

I never felt to push or shove people toward the God of love.
It seemed that it was not my place, just give them time and give
them space."

But then I came to understand when vision of a failing dam
appeared in revelation's dream, and as I dreamt I looked to see

a town that lay downstream below. In dead of night, they did not know
that little time remained until collapse would come and floods would fill

the valley, bringing death to all the sleeping souls, and so I called
as loud as I could raise my voice. I ran the streets, I had no choice.

I beat upon windows and doors. I warned of what things lay in store.
I begged them, "please rise up and leave!" But many simply looked at me

as though I were a crazy fool. Some slammed their door, and some
were cruel.
Some mocked me as they turned away, and I had no more time to stay

for in the distance, I could hear the raging flood that now was near.
Thus, all that I could do was flee to higher ground for my safety.

Then as I turned and looked back down, a wall of water swept the town
with total devastating force. I cried out loud. My heart remorsed.

If only they had known the cost, but they are gone, so many lost.
And so, I learned from that night's dream I do not have the luxury

to sit and let the time wane thin. The time is now, I must begin
to warn as many as I can.... for soon shall come The Son of Man.

A BIRD NOW GONE

No bird remains to sing his song,
so silence pounds the whole day long.

In beat with memory of the day
I clapped to make him go away.

The fault, it clearly lies with me,
the bird was what the bird should be.

Now I live knowing I was wrong…
to want to silence any song.

Reference 'A Minor Bird' by Robert Frost

STRANGE FRIENDS

I was a stranger, you took me in,
but I found you were stranger still.
I guess we're two peas in a pod
cuz neither of us fits the bill
of all the many ways the world expects
two blokes like us to be.
You took me in, now we've become…
the strangest friends you'll ever see.

WALK AWAY

I wonder.
I wonder.
I wonder why it goes.
I deny it,
try to fight it
against the way it flows.

I ignore it.
I deplore it,
try to push it far away.
But I fear it,
I'm too near it
and it haunts me every day.

For circling in the skies are things
I wish I could disguise,
that melt to crystal teardrops
and it makes me realize -

that I'm part of it,
not above it.
No, I'm not the way I was.
Oh, I hate it,
execrate it
and everything it does.

So, I'll change it,
rearrange it,
try to start another day.
Then I'll stop it.
Yeah, I'll stop it…
and I'll turn and walk away.

PIECE THAT IS MISSING

The piece that is missing
is the piece of my heart,
that I threw like a stone
when our love fell apart.

Without looking I threw it
as far as I could.
Now I'm stuck with the fact...
that I've lost it for good.

ALONE

I wish it would have been a war
that was the explanation for
the reason you are not around,
the reason I don't hear the sound
of your voice anymore.
No, I don't hear it anymore.

And I wish it were all a dream
although a bad one it would seem,
cuz then at least I'd have the chance
to open up my eyes and glance
upon your face, but I don't see it.
No, not anymore.

And I wish there were reasons why
no chance was given for goodbye.
A day, a flash and you were gone.
Now lonely days roll on and on
where I don't have you anymore.
No, nothing anymore.

So I wish something else were the
explanation given me
for why I'm left inside this empty home.
But I suppose there isn't one.
It's over and what's done is done.
There's nothing now. Yes… I am all alone.

RELAPSE

The state of the worse. The state of the damned.
Is this the sad state where I find that I am?

The evil inside me who long dwelt therein,
I'd given him home for he felt like a friend.

But then cast I did he out of necessity
to walk in dry places, where rest he did seek.

And while he did roam, I set forth alone
acting quickly to sweep and to garnish my home.

Till at last it did seem to be ornate and clean,
and I said to myself, "I am finally free!"

But then after a time when no rest he could find,
he turned back to my home that was clean and refined.

As he studied to know in what state it might be,
he stood there and smiled, for he found it empty.

Then he quick turned about with a wave of his hand,
calling seven more like him to join in his plan

where they all entered in with a mindset to stay.
Thus, I cannot believe at the end of the day

how I've come to arrive in this state where I am.
The state of the worse… the state of the damned.

Ref: Matthew 12: 43-45

A FINAL NOTE

First note chimes,
long silence gone.
Like breath again,
or light at dawn.

Pure joy to hear,
healed by each note.
Lost in the melody,
finding hope.

With new life comes
new eyes to see,
and ears to hear
but eventually

the song winds down,
fire fades to smoke.
For each song has…
a final note.

END OF THE DREAM

Look there and tell me,
what do you see?
A darkening sky filled with fire.
A fall into black holes,
circling the things
that make up your every desire.

Look now and tell me,
just how will this go
when you reach to grasp it again?
You'll feel it disintegrate,
dirt covered snow
leaves not but the mire in the end.

Yes, look now and add it up,
where does this end?
A story book finish 'twould seem.
A final, "I told you so",
check the last box…
and come to the end of the dream.

70 TIMES 7

Unto what shall I liken my struggle filled walk in life?
Unto a breath without air, gasping and grasping
for that which I can clearly see and ever try to be,
but like unto the shining stars of heaven's glory above -
lies as it would seem high above my reach.

Yet my hands are stretched heavenward.

Unto what shall I compare the hope which I have for change?
To the light of sun above the storm, breaking through betimes
with the brilliance of a gleam and a glimpse of the dream,
but even as the delicate flower of the desert plain -
it withers and returns to the ground hidden once again from view.

Yet my faith awaits the rains of spring.

And what likeness portrays my will to go on?
The waves of the wind driven sea ever striving to come ashore,
yet each time falling back for gravity they lack.
But like the shimmering beauty of the freshly fallen snow -
though it turns to grey and melts away yet, is destined to come
again.

So also, am I resolved to return in the season and never surrender...
until seventy times seven.

DON'T GET ME STARTED

Once in a while I hear words that just grab me.
Most times I let'em go by, but some get past me.
Seconds turn into hours, so I live in slow motion.
Dive deep into words, words as deep as the ocean.
Things I've wanted to say since the day that we parted.
Want to let it all out but... don't get me started.

Everything spinning round in my mind,
millions of strings I keep wound up inside.
Tied up in knots on the inside, it happens.
I tie them up just because they are snappin'.
Can't hold it back so it seeps out in rhymes,
piece mail the pieces and bits of my mind.
Bite through my tongue, I know I gotta filter it.
Have to because I know no one can handle it.

Done doing that, gonna let it all flow.
Look at yourself, tell me what do we know?
Can anyone say that they know who we are?
Blinded because we think we've come so far.
Really? That's nonsense, you still gotta ask it,
"Despite it all don't we end up in a casket?"

We're as blind as we've ever been,
dumbed down with pride.
Thinking technology sits on our side.
Thinking we know, but it's nothing but shit!
Wipe the smile from you're face because...
you're missing it.

Now I know what you think, "turn him off, walk away."
"Another loudmouth who's got too much to say."
Maybe so but I'm calling you out this one time.
Open your heart and you'll learn from this rhyme.
Look in the mirror, this time finally see in.
Look in your eyes, do you know where you've been?
You're still there, you never left, don't think you did.
Blacked it all out before you were a kid.

Most people think there must be more than this.
Thinking there's not's really quite ludicrous,
but so are the thoughts of the ones who believe.
Religion and science make no sense to me
because neither one goes where the truth fully lies.
Stuck in the argument. Stuck on their sides.
Thinking to trust what they hold in their hands.
Thinking they know what the hell God has planned.
Thinking their senses give credence at all.
Living in bubbles and thinking so small.

Science believes that their craft gives a way.
Churches give what amounts to Novocain.
High-minded IQs that think there's no God.
Closed-mind believers who stay in the fog.
Both have the truth right in front of their view,
but truth will destroy everything they both do
so, they stay on their sides both defending their ways.
Stuck in their viewpoints and lost in the haze.

Only the ones who resist this whole fraud
have any chance of discovering God.
But if they resist then they will also find -
everything comes through the heart and the mind.
The mind grows by light and the heart lives by love.
A continuous stream of both comes from above,
giving joy to the heart and truth to the mind.
But it is too easy to miss these I find
for there's near endless cares meant to cover them up.
Endless distractions and if that's not enough,
everything's tied to money so that in the end,
light and love have little chance to get in.

And what of our knowledge of just who we are?
We don't even know what we're made of thus far.
They keep zooming in and keep finding each time,
matter's made of something that's too small to find.
And that will not change, they can search til they die.
It's a snipe hunt of sorts for there's nothing to find.
At least not of which can be found with the eye,
nor with the five senses and do you know why?
Because there's a God, it's as simple as that.
From there it adds up if you follow the facts,
and drop all conclusions that ever have been.
The rest is pure logic, you'll find in the end -
intelligence is all there is that is real,
the things we experience and what we feel.

So, love and light are the most valuable things
because the experience that they both bring
gives joy to the heart and truth to the mind,
and that is enough I think you will find.
For time's an illusion as is all of space.
The universe lies right in front of your face,
but we all seem to miss it, we all make the err -
we trust in the things that we think we find here.

If you ever can finally let it all go
and see with faith, not with eyes then you will know,
that you're a God too, at least one meant to be.
But only if somehow… you will finally see.

MIDNIGHT CITY

Now the calm of new fallen snow
lies in silent peace and stillness,
gently covering the loneliness
of midnight city streets.

As I walk, I cannot help but wonder.

How can it be so unaware
of where it present lies?
Has it not seen the desolation?
Has it not heard the cries?

Perhaps it doesn't know the tales,
lying there on unkept ground
on the broken streets and walkways
and rooftops all around.

But I suppose I too am unaware,
lost in the moment.

For on morrow day when snow melts away,
and peaceful white turns back to grey,
my nightly walk shall once again be
amidst the tranquil cold
of midnight city streets.

But for now I pray,
let the impression of this night
rest upon my heart forever, knowing...
that God truly is no respecter of men.

A STEP HALF MADE

As lightening shone and thunder blew,
I danced the dance that dancers do.

They danced it back and asked if I
would mind them dancing through the night.

I thought no harm could come of this
besides, such company I've missed.

Thus, on we danced so unaware
that torrent rains beyond compare

fell down in floods on higher ground,
and like a wall came crashing down.

Then somewhere in a step half made
the dance I danced was washed away.

Now all that's left for you to see -
remains of the catastrophe.

Oh, hopefully from this you'll know…
don't ever dance when thunder blows.

CHICKEN EVERY MEAL

I get a little tired of it - folks who seem to think
they must be happy all the time or else they're on the brink
of some traumatic end, oh yes, like everything is bad
if once in a blue moon they have to deal with being sad.

It makes no sense to me at all. Just what do they expect,
they should be happy day and night and never get set back?
Well, I can't grasp it, not at all. In fact, is makes me ill
to contemplate if happiness my every moment filled.

To me that is the same as eating chicken every meal.
Why would I want that? God forbid! It simply isn't real
to think you can be happy if that's all you ever know.
You can't, so just relax a bit… and let your feelings flow.

SELF INFLICTED

Looking out from deep inside
this fortress here wherein I hide.
Formed brick by brick in rounds of pain,
some circumstantial, others made
by hand selecting from the first -
fine crafted moldings of the worst.

With clays of pity, doubt and fear,
mix in the water, make it clear
so all around will go away.
Form isolation day by day
til self-inflicted world of one
is all that's left, the fortress done.

Now every brick formed tells a tale
of how I crafted out this hell,
where trapped inside I live alone...
my self-inflicted one-man home.

THE DAY AFTER

It's different now,
all the world around
cloaked in grey,
yet cool in the shadow.
Void of sound,
yet comfortable,
quiet,
reliable,
predictable,
sure.

Yes, things are very different…
on the day after you give up on your dreams.

ALMOST THERE FOR YOU

Sailed an ocean just to reach you,
passed through a hurricane or two,
hit land to find a ring upon your hand.
I was almost there for you.

Crossed a continent to find you,
every hardship I passed through,
at ocean's rim you were there with him.
I was almost there for you.

Does it pay to lay your heart on the line,
or believe that true love's true?
Now I spend my time traveling on, I'm fine...
I was almost there for you.

FREEDOM

Why do we always end up in the place where we began?
Why is it freedom fades away and dies in every land?

I think the problem lies within the reason why we fight,
for it is not to win the war then stand guard day and night

with vigilance. No sadly this is not the cause at all,
and so the stage is set that every time we rise we fall.

Yes, time has shown we do not fight to make sure we stay free.
No, rather we fight for the chance… to live our lives at ease.

NO MATTER

How many times must a man come to grips
with all of the troubles in life,
where voyages tend to become sunken ships
and seems every path leads to strife?

How often must he try, despite what he sees,
a battle that's too big to win?
Where forces are meant to bring him to his knees
and make him start over again.

How many times when rock bottom he's reached
and no light above finds his eyes,
will he fight to gather the words he's heard preached,
declaring that he's meant to rise?

What is the potential of a man who won't quit,
who holds fast to all that he knows?
There's power to change the whole world where he stands
if he goes on… despite how it goes.

RECKONING

Once sat upon a waveless ocean,
time stood still for lack of motion.
No one spoke for all could see
the guardians of eternity.

Then water slowly turned to glass
ablaze with fire, no soul could pass.
And all knew time at last did bring...
the final day of reckoning.

ONE MISSING

I want to write a song today from six feet under here.
Won't paint to kill the dead saints but I want to make it clear
that I've been praying in the dark while lying in this grave,
and wishing the bathwater clean in hopes that it can save.

I hope to finally find the strength. I know I have to try,
but so far every effort yields the gist of one big lie.
That's why I'm here, I've learned there is no X amount of words
that have the power to change despite how many I have heard.

But I know I'm the one who has to claw my up through
this dirt room I have called my home, it's time for me to do
whatever it takes can't you see, the end is at the door?
I want to rise and feel that I'm not broken anymore.

Cuz everything is changed by time, why should I die alone?
Why shouldn't I break through this ground, rise up and make a home?
So I will write a song today as if I were a king,
then you will know, "I won't let go" by every word I sing.

CIRCLES

Got circles in my mind,
but words don't help me find,
so I stare at the world to watch it spin.
Got circles in my mind,
in the pond of space and time
I cast in stones to make the waves begin.

Thoughts weaving through the universe,
I always wonder which is worse -
to understand or think you do when blind?
It seems to me the polls are in
with ignorance a lock to win
because it is the default every time.

So I keep contemplating things,
and what all this someday will bring
when really all the circles make it clear.
In the grand scheme it's just a blip,
too small to even notice it,
but from our view it's everything, I fear.

LIFELONG FRIEND

When all the leaves fall from the trees,
what does it mean to you and me?
Perhaps it wasn't meant to be
as now we reach the end.

Is there some place we didn't go?
We tried every fork in the road,
and never seemed to find a home.
My dear, what's at the end?

But we're ok. Yeah, certainly
we could have done things differently.
But side by side we took this ride
and so what is to gain,

by dwelling on what could have been,
and looking back time and again
at what we didn't have -
what's there to gain?

But rather let's just you and I
enjoy what we have left and try
to make the most of it
my lifelong friend.

Because all that matters now is we
are still together, can't you see.
That's all that's ever mattered...
in the end.

NOT A SINGLE THING

At the end of the day if the truth be told,
we don't own a single thing we hold.
Not the spoils we gain, nor the gold in hand.
Not the things we reap. Not the tracks of land
that we build upon, where we stake our claim.
Not the talents held, nor the claims to fame.
Not the words we write. Not the songs we sing.
No, we don't own a single thing.
But the will we hold deep inside our heart.
Yes, the choice we make, that's the only part
of our whole existence that we own,
which is ours to give and ours alone.

For we cannot make one hair black or white.
We can't turn back time. We can't stop the night
when the setting sun brings our time to go,
leaving all behind. Brother, don't you know
that the time wanes short, not a day to waste?
Time to realize why we're in this place.
We are stewards of everything that is ours.
Ours to use for better or for worse.
It's a final test, may the record bare -
that we made a choice… and we chose to share.

WHAT COMES OF DREAMS

Oh, why so many dreams bestowed
in young and tender years,
fall into drifting dust decay
then sadly disappear.

Are dreams to blame for broken hearts
and quiet hour's remorse?
Or is the dreamer born of guilt
for veering from its course?

Are dreams unfair for rising up
to skies in brilliant hue?
Perhaps they take no time for thought
and ask too much to do.

But would a dream be such a thing
if every hand could reach?
What treasure would it bring to bare?
What lesson would it teach?

Oh, grant I pray that I should never
stand amongst the crowd,
and watch with idle faithless feet
while mundane cares enshroud.

No, I will dare to dream above
midst Heaven's brilliant streams,
and quiet vigil watch and keep
til come... what comes of dreams.

HOW SHE SEES

Light…
what a beautiful light.
If only to touch for a moment
as day turns to night.

And how…
how I wish it could it be,
we all could see through eyes of children
so innocently.

Oh, see how she glows
from her head to her toes
as the light gleams from her face.
Will we change how she sees,
or change so we see things her way?

Will we change how she sees,
or change so we see things her way?

HUMBUG

I can't stand another year of this
with the sales that start after summer's bliss,
and the songs that play round the clock each day,
and the gosh darn ice and snow.

And the ho ho ho's, and the jingle bells,
and the wasted time - makes me mad as hell!
And crowds that block every road and shop
every dog-gone place I go!

No, I can't stand so much as another day.
Wish this time of year would just go away,
and leave me here to my mansion warm and snug.

Cuz I'm tired of the groans and the chains that creak,
and those three damn ghosts who won't let me sleep.
So to you and them I say... BAH HUMBUG!

THE CLOCK

There's a heart that beats
and a clock that chimes.
Moments pass as they both keep time.

Opportunities lost again.
Words don't flow from an idle pen.
Deeds don't come from an idle hand.
Seeds won't grow in a barren land.

Something stalks me, something's there.
Something haunts my every prayer.

Aggravation, life slips by.
Desperation, sleepless nights.

Cold against the words I say.
Time won't make this go away.
It merely ticks to count the deeds.
Mounting numbers don't mislead.

They all add up to tell the tale
of downward slide towards the hell
that I've created. Idle hands.
Not but dust on barren land
depicts the seeds that I have sown,
and with this pen I'm left alone
in idle silence. Years go by...
as the heart beats on
and the clock keeps time.

BLUE SUNSHINE

The words have fallen silent now and dreams passed away.
The pills have taken over and I don't know what to say.

My bags have all been packed for me. The driver waits impatiently.
Not car nor driver fits this mystic land.
The hallway doors each filled with they who's eyes plead out for me
to stay,
it hurts to see they do not understand.

I never will forget my time amongst these friends of song and rhyme.
They'll always hold a place inside my heart.
But time has passed, I've given in and let the pressure finally win -
"You have to fix the world you tore apart."

And so, I tread this path I took. Once in the car a final look -
such hidden beauty few shall ever know.
Then view dissolves to rising dust. A cold inside, a stagnant must,
another pill will get me where I go.

Yes, words have fallen silent now. No longer is there rhyme.
No longer is there light except... the light of blue sunshine.

BY THE WELL

Twas an ordinary scene on an ordinary day,
she an ordinary woman on her ordinary way.
Doing work of little consequence, she walked to Jacob's Well.
Could she have known that someday all would know her tale?

For as she went to fill her pot a man she noticed there,
who were he any other Jew would not have stopped to care.
But he took time and bid her, "Dip the cup and give me drink",
and from this she knew that he did not think others think.

For her home was of Samaria. Her people often shunned,
but in a quiet voice he spoke and soon her trust he won.
For he told her all the things that in her life she ever did,
then spoke of living waters and he offered her this bid –
that if she would partake of such she'd never thirst again.
To this she answered, "Give me thus so I can worship then".

But in response he answered with a phrase to stand all time -
"ye worship… ye know not what", a haunting truth sublime.
For every living soul must also face this thought as they
grow up from adolescence into life to make their way.
The scriptures challenge all that Life Eternal is to know
the one true God who dwells on high, yet we live here below.

And with no way to see him, touch his hand, or hear his voice,
the stage is thereby set that every sole must make the choice:
to heed his invitation – "plant the seed of faith and try
the words that have been given of the prophets by and by".
"And see if not the tree doth grow by study and by prayer,
as your load lightens when you trust to cast on me your care".

So now I write to ask myself as well as each of you,
do you know the one you worship, do you know the God that's true?
The sands of time are running thin, the day is at the door
when we'll see him face to face… and face our answers evermore.

HOW HEAVEN

It seems that life's a limbo so if eternity is as well,
it's hard to not conclude that every outcome will be hell.

For everything we do, in time fades into mundane dust.
The shiny steel of bliss today each next day gains more rust.

So how can Heaven hold its awe when eons pass like days?
For golden streets walked once too oft seem normal in their ways.

There must be more to God on high and in where he resides
than lasting life and majesty in worlds above the skies.

What could explain Heaven above and the eternal joy it gives?
The secret lies in what God does… not in the place he lives.

PURE WATER

A life sustained by water pure,
yet marred by memory of the wine.
Like fragrant waft of soft allure
diminished not by hands of time.

Forever clear the water streams,
yet never ends the draw to wine.
Forever helpless so all seems
to purge the memory from my mind.

Though water's healing - ever constant,
soft and clean and unaware
how often it hath quenched my thirst
and oft hath left me standing there.

A gaze in awe and silent yearning,
watching how the water flows.
Mesmerized by every trickle,
wishing I could just let go

of every string the wine has woven
through the fabric of my soul.
Doth feel betimes a fact well proven -
I've not the will to let it go.

For wine is strong to those who drink
and feel the fire of liquor's hold.
Changed thus forever so I think,
in moment's time my future sold.

But hold I fast to water's beauty,
resolute despite all time.
Let God and angel's bear this witness…
I choose water over wine.

SAVOR

Spent another day chasing like each day before,
and what did it gain us this time?
It feels like we're racing against a short clock,
in effort to scavenge a dime.

I guess I don't get it - the purpose of such,
seems not but to gather in barns.
A quest to arrive at a distant mirage
with no thought of what the quest harms.

Do we consider, what else could be
if we had a much higher cause?
There's so much we don't have, potential is lost
because we are living at odds.

With the Joneses competing, and nature depleting
as we swim through envy and strife.
And we've tied all to paper and took all the flavor...
that should be the savor in life.

ONE CHANGE

I wish I could teach the world one simple thing,
then pray that they grasp it and start following.

Because it would change every outcome to be,
dispel all the darkness and set the soul free.

'Twould make everything we do under the sun
a pure joy to do just because of this one

simple change that has nothing to do with the things
that we spend our time doing, no that's not the thing.

But rather the change I wish each soul would try -
don't change what you're doing... change the reason why.

IN TRANCE

It feels so deep,
enchanted sleep.
A haunting spirit.
Eyes to weep.

With trembling hand
stretched forth to feel,
yet nothing felt.
Five hearts of steel.

Creep closer, closer,
closing in.
In staggered breath
as night begins.

Where mystic songs
will have their way.
Hypnotic rhythm,
come what may.

No presence here.
No ties abound.
No turning back.
No solid ground.

Just voices, voices
from the deep.
Just voices now…
forever sleep.

REFLECTION

I woke up this morning to the drip drop of rain,
then lie there just thinking how peaceful it was.
Wrapped in the moment, reflecting again
how totally different my life is because

I long ago finally came to myself,
I guess you could say like the prodigal son -
deciding to put errant ways on the shelf,
and live life for something a bit more than fun.

I lie there just thinking as minutes rolled by,
with each tic of time a new memory sprang
until I was overwhelmed, tears filled my eyes...
to the tic toc of time, and the drip drop of rain.

THE EYE OF THE STORM

Once crashed the waves in tempest's storm,
and blew the wind as sails were torn.
Once drove the rain against frozen skin
as darkness took the vessel in.

Once void of any hope at all,
trapped deep inside the prison's wall,
beneath the crushing weight of lead
but faintest light shown from ahead.

Then in a moment, skies were clear
and ocean's calm dispelled the fear.
It seemed blue skies meant all is well.
The storm has past now mend the sail.

So gave I way to those who care,
and bent the knee and found what's there -
pure wine upon the lees in hand
and from it, strength to make a stand.

But drifting time brought slumber's sleep
as wind reversed across the deep.
Blue sky gave way to churning black.
Nowhere to go, no turning back.

For little deeds allowed back in
like seeds of tares took root again
and oh, how fast the vines did grow.
And I had nowhere left to go.

Once back again in tempest's hold.
Now worse the winds, now worse the cold.
The brief blue sky and radiant warm…
was only the eye of the storm.

WHEN THE DARKNESS FALLS

It's colder now and seems somehow
more empty than before.
I wish I'd known the future then,
and what it held in store.
No longer is there will of heart
to venture form these walls,
and so I sit alone inside...
when the darkness falls.

Each stone hand crafted for the cause
to block away the pain.
The mortar mixed to guarantee
no feeling will remain.
A mist enshrouds the inner grounds,
with siren's voice it calls.
To comfort as I drift within...
when the darkness falls.

A subtle shift and weightless drift
are all that's left to feel.
No sign of any signs of life,
no sense of what is real.
Just drifting, drifting ever on
down never-ending halls.
Forever locked inside my head...
when the darkness falls.

NAÏVE

Naive enough to believe that it's true –
the world spins around the old red, white and blue.

God set it up, and so surely it's his.
He'll keep it forever, I'm sure his plan is

to return some fine day and then next I suppose,
he'll start a campaign and go after your vote.

He'll take out some ads and he'll put up some signs.
He'll make lofty promises, "Things will be fine!"

"As soon as I'm President, Heaven will come."
"Just give me your vote and the rest will be done."

Can't you see just how foolish the thought of this is,
for when he returns, he will take what is his –

the keys of the kingdom and throne to this world.
All life living under a new flag unfurled.

So as the end nears just remember one thing,
Christ isn't a president... he is a king.

BLIND

Blind keepers,
mind readers,
throw them in the pod.
Make them think they have a way
to see through all the fog.

Let them start with nothing,
they'll grow up and think they've won.
Set the stage so from the play
they'll add things one by one.

They'll come up with conclusions
thinking they've figured it out,
and all the while just watch them…
cuz that's what it's all about.

SAME OLD SONG

The torn remain
of what was plain
waves now ore frozen ground,
in winds that blow
cold ice and snow
and other feelings down.

There isn't much
left in a touch
to calm the trembling hand.
For winter's chill
falls colder still
in cloak across the land.

The settled dust
and cankered rust
guard safe against the grain,
while fading dim
from deep within
gives root to growing pain.

How did it go
from there to here?
How could it end so wrong?
A love once whole,
two lives once full…
yet still the same old song.

SIDES OF THE COIN

The battle before us -
"The Left and The Right",
calling to everyone,
"Join in the fight!"

Calling, demanding -
"Which side are you on?"
The Left or The Right
not the right or the wrong.

Dividing while fighting
not missing a day.
Not doing or proving
they mean what they say.

A dog and a pony
make up their whole show,
crafted to hide
where they want us to go.

Crafted to hide
who is really behind
all that we're seeing,
and someday we'll find

that The Left and The Right
who call all men to join...
are nothing but opposite
sides of the coin.

SECRETS

A million things swimming around in my head.
Things I could say that should never be said.

Things I could tell that you'd never believe.
Things that I've seen that are too far to see.

Things that I've heard that are not made of sound.
Things that I know which have never been found.

Things that could change the world. Things that could heal.
Things that would terrify were they revealed.

Things of the type based on all that I've seen,
are best left unspoken and kept in between

myself and the one who has shown them to me.
The one who keeps whispering continually.

In my mind they're all swimming, an ocean too vast
to contain it all so… I'll risk all that have.

ONLINE BEST WHO?

I can see it in your eyes from across the room,
makes my heart ache, it's a mistake - why do you
compare the self-view, dark-hue worst of yourself
to the online best of who?

Gosh dammit! I can't stand it! If I had a single wish -
open windows, heal the widows and the few.
Those who give it all away, feel they fail some way
to the online best of who.

Wanna burn it to the ground, plow it under, put it down,
help you understand your beauty from my view.
Cuz it's all a bunch of shit, give it up, don't look at it…
yeah, the online best of who.

SHOW ME THE WAY

Someone had to show me the way,
though much of the time I just followed mine
so you watched from the distance, I know.
But it's clear to me now, wish I'd seen it somehow
and done more to make sure that you know -

your example means more than the whole world to me,
for you stood your whole life for what's true.
Yeah, somebody had to show me the way...
Mom, I'm grateful that person was you.

THE GATHERER

The Gatherer and the Giver sat atop a hill to gaze again
down at the village where they lived, and talk about the ones in need.
At end of day as sun went down, they sat there talking in the dim
as soul by soul they contemplated what was the best way to feed.

They did this often for they knew, despite the many years gone by,
the need to gather and to give would always be in high demand.
But on this eve the Giver took the time to ask the Gatherer why
he worked so hard behind the scenes. The Giver didn't understand.

For he was ever in the light, the one who all the people saw
taking what he had received and giving to the ones in need,
sharing in the joy it brings (it was the best part of the job).
But his friend never got this chance because he made the choice to lead

a quite life of gathering. A life of no fanfare at all.
So when the Giver asked him why he toiled so hard to gather in,
he sat a while just thinking as he watched the evening shadows fall,
not quite sure how to answer for the thought had never came to him.

So when he finally spoke his words fit well into the sunset night.
Soft and slow, the words as natural as the scene before their view -
"I do it for deep in my heart the Spirit tells me that it's right,
for I am given everything that passes through my hands to you."

WHAT I'VE LEARNED

They struggle to know how I feel,
yet each question they ask only makes it more real.

And they search for a way to get in.
Hell, the door isn't locked, it just blocked from within.

They remember the way that I was.
Well big deal, so do I and I don't know the cause.

And they ask it again and again,
"Why can't you be you back before this began?"

Don't they think that I would if I could?
Well, I'm sorry I don't act the way that I should.

So the stage is now set to go on,
everyone join together to point out what's wrong.

Cuz together they're sure they can win,
helping me learn how to live once again

But the only thing I've learned instead -
if ya gotta be sick… don't be sick in the head.

CONFLICTION

Balancing midst them both, two lives at once. Split down the middle and torn at the seams.
Tiptoe the balance beam, pleasing the ones who know only one side of things.

Confliction, a way of life down to the core. From every angle, two people 'twould seem.
Not yet discovered a way to be more, so both lives are not but a dream.

Illusions, acts on stage, fulfilling roles. Wondering how it would be.
Letting it melt to one, fill in the holes, and finally just become me.

I wish it were simply that simple to do, but both sides are set in their way, and fully expect me to be the one who they need at the end of the day.

But only so far can a double life go before the stretch tears you in two.
And you cannot hide the blood, everyone knows... but no one knows quite what to do.

DAUGHTER OF GOD

You're not what you think.
Things aren't as they seem.
Lived your whole life
against what you believe.
I know that it's hard not to
look at yourself
feeling like you are lost,
could have been something else.

Feeling like there's no hope
given all that you've done,
like there's no way back to
the light of the sun.
But trust me, that's bullshit,
a literal fraud!
The truth is you're precious…
a daughter of God.

HE COULD HAVE

He could have come to rule the world,
he should have been a king.
He could have had all that he want,
but then what would it bring?

For he knew who he was and also
what the world would need.
Thus, he chose life a poor man's son
who lived a life to bleed

upon the cross, between two thieves,
completely left alone.
'Twould seem at glance a failure
in this world with heart of stone.

But in that very thought
the answer lies, "why did he do?"
He didn't live his life for him...
he lived his life for you.

SHALLOW BREATH

Soft moonlit eyes that paralyze.
Unbridled passion on the rise.
The room afire in fading light.
Fragrant desire fills up the night.

As worlds dissolve, so unaware.
Entangled in your casual stare.
Nowhere to hide. No way to see.
No self-control inside of me.

Slow motion moves through tangled time.
In shallow breath I feel that I'm
adrift upon your velvet sea…
your captive for eternity.

THE GRIND

I must have wished a thousand times
that somehow we could live our lives
for something more.

And I can't help but wonder why
we strive to keep so much in line,
what is it for?

Can't you see we spend our time
building what we call "The Grind",
finding ways to numb the pain it causes.
Blind leading the blind.

Can't you see we spend our time
building what we call "The Grind".
What is it for?

MOMENTS

Picture frame the moments.
In diaries write them down.
Hold on to such with all you have
for times will come around,
when they will be all that you have
to make it one more day.
And on that day let all else go…
then you will find the way.

ONE CELL

Run
as fast as you can.
Red shades of dismal
flowing fear
melt to the glass of sand.

Hide
in the hollow hidden dry.
Drink down the spell
of earth and hell
indifferent to the sky.

Lie
forever un-seamed.
Face down amidst
the death of sound,
black holes of melody.

Sleep
to the blood of setting sun.
From spiral dreams
look down at what...
one cell has now become.

B'JANGLED TOURETTE'S

Bah ratcha tas contavalaz
you rase-neflapher'd wagicaud!
Condaver haufin polysnip!
I'll tell you just where you can stick
your pi-calogin traginine!
You heard me right you doboline.
Go rosigate your dodgisnap
you traginated jollipap!
Xysnerf neflected nillidip!
Take that YOU LILLY ARKABLIP!
COE SNAZE I-CAVIN WAJALLAY!!
BI-ROPKI LISHNIF DOBIKAY!!!
FLANT-AG-LACATED HYBOLEE!!!!…

Uhm…

Why is everyone looking at me?

ALL THAT WILL REMAIN

Always searching for the next good time
and what the world can bring.
Always looking for the next big deal
and what it's offering.

Never thinking very far ahead
or worrying about the cost.
Never wanting much to understand
or caring what gets lost.

Always thinking I don't need to change,
believing that I'm fine.
Always doing what I want to do
and taking what is mine.

Never listening to their advice,
for surely they don't know.
Never going to let them think I'm down,
or I'm out of control.

Always needing more to get the fix
and more to pay the price.
Always promising I'll give it up,
my own strength will suffice.

Never thought that things would be this way.
Won't let them know the cause.
Never going to let myself admit
the damage that it does.

Always going through the cycle.
Always starting up again.
Always finding out the hard way
that there's just no way to win.

Never going stop the bleeding
or the guilt or all the pain,
so the shell of me that people see...
is all that will remain.

NEXT IN LINE

It feels kinda like someone gave me a drug,
mixed for the purpose of stamping out love.

Slipped like a Mickey when I was away.
Slammed down the hatch and now all I can say

is, "I don't know why I feel nothing at all."
Head like a hammer straight into the wall.

Black coat of tar dripping straight from my heart.
Struggle for breath while still acting the part.

Things that I've relished no longer seem fun.
Trapped in a cycle but still on the run.

Live for a purpose without any goals.
Watching it slip away as I get old.

Talks with myself and with all who will hear.
None seem to understand and so I fear,

I'm destined to fall, then perhaps they will learn
I was next in line... and 'twas simply my turn.

PRAYER OF THE MODERN DAY PHARISEE

Sinners & publicans. Pharisees, scribes.
Unto neither of these could I ever subscribe,
for I read of these groups in the scriptures each day
and both make me feel to exclaim when I pray:

"Oh praise be that I'm not as other men are,
like those sinners and publicans, God keep me far
from their damnable words and their damnable deeds,
and more so than this, Oh God keep me free
from those scribes and those pharisees, they above all
are the worst kind of people and destined to fall.
Oh Lord I pray – keep me apart from these men,
and I promise my life will go on as it's been -
fasting two times a week, paying tithes of my gain,
doing all that I do, but I need not explain
for Thou knowest all this. Yes, the time has come when
I must wrap this prayer up and close with amen."

No, I'll never be like anyone from those tribes,
not like sinners and publicans, pharisees, scribes.
For I'm nothing like them. No, my time is well spent!
Me, a just soul who has… no need to repent.

Reference:
Luke 18: 10-14
Luke 15:7

EMPTY SEATS

Take a church full of sinners with issues galore,
each needing profoundly the grace of the Lord.

Some trapped in addiction, some weighed down in sin,
some struggling with faith, some who tried but gave in.

Some filled with anger and some with regret,
some who cannot forgive, but there's one group I fret -

the judgmental crowd. They make it so tough,
thinking they have no sin or that they're good enough.

And I wish that were all but it's not for I find,
they poison the whole for they're willfully blind.

Doing all that they must to protect the charade,
ranking sins amongst others and handing out shame.

Handcrafting a culture that turns out to be,
in direct opposition to what sinners need.

A place to be open, a place to confess,
a place to find comfort, a place to find rest.

A place to find Christ and the healing He gives.
A place to start over, but somehow this lives

in the culture of church after church I observe.
I guess human nature just can't be deterred.

For it seems to be common despite where I go -
the part poisons all, no one stops it and so

the judgmental crowd wins and history repeats
where they end up the only ones... left in the seats.

SUNSET MEMORY

An old porch swing made once for two.
Cool night breeze calling out to you.
Ten thousand memories rise above,
the sunset waters of our love.

Just like the day slips into the night,
the love we had that was oh so right
it slipped away. It slipped away,
like day slips into night.

Was our love doomed to come and pass,
one day as fire, one day as ash?
Night after night. Night after night,
the memory of your face.

Yeah, was our loved doomed to come and pass,
one day as fire, one day as ash?
Night after night, I'm left to trace…
the sunset memory of your face.

NO ARRIVAL

I charted once a course to gold,
a place wherein I might take hold
of everything I ever wished.
Retire there, enjoy the bliss.

But every time I thought that I
was finally there, I'd stop and try
to take my rest and grab the things
that I expected such to bring.

But each time I found to my dread,
the land of gold lay still ahead.
And on and on this cycle went
until at last my strength was spent.

It left me standing in despair,
afraid I'd never make it there.
Frustrated to the very core
and wondering just what life is for.

"Does not this journey have an end?"
"Perhaps the gold is just pretend."
But then so soft inside my head
the voice of reason spoke and said,

"The reason why you can't arrive…
you want what's on the other side."

NOT THERE BEFORE

You saved them but then fell again,
the circle's in the sky.
Divided fence and happenstance
don't care if it's a lie.

Tomorrow's way fades into grey
and blue melts into black,
as silent sounds in crushing rounds
creep in for the attack.

An empty stage and crumpled page
bleed deep into your brain.
Don't ever sleep. Don't ever weep.
Don't ever feel the pain.

This same old room, familiar gloom.
The same old window's stare.
As tears rain down, disfigured clown.
Why should you even care?

But something new, not there before
won't let you go away...
A million voices fill the air.
A million voices pray.

CAPTAIN, MY CAPTAIN

The wind seems to blow when the cold settles in.
Darkness will fall after shadows begin.
The end truly came long before you were through,
now everyone is going to miss you.

Captain, my captain now gone to the sky.
Words can't describe all the reasons we cry.
The circle's complete now, there's no reason why.
Captain, my captain… goodbye.

…Tribute Robin Williams

SILHOUETTES

Death transcends the toll of time.
Stands beneath a smoke-filled sky.
Spirits rise up from the past,
row by row from first to last.

Like silhouettes of lifeless trees
against the sun, no foot can flee.
Then sink they into desert sand…
as hate consumes the life of man.

QUIET NOW

You sit there rocking,
no more people talking,
drifting with the wind across the grain.
It's peaceful like you planned it.
No one make's demands it's
quiet now and every day's the same.

It's a shame
that something pure and free,
became a ball and chain tied to misery.
Like an island separate from the land,
the waters made you miss the life you planned.

So you sit there rocking,
the voices that once talked to you have all...
withered away.

Was it the hardness
or something in your veins
that never let hold the things you own?
Just like you sip black coffee
but hate the taste,
you block the world away
but hate to be alone.

Such a shame
that something meant to be,
blinded you to what you could have seen.
Now you know
what you were looking for
was just a winding road toward a closing door.

So sit there rocking
with no more people talking,
drifting with the grain…
whichever way the wind blows.

The Clover Tune
Mandolin Orange

SILENT FLIGHT

What lies beneath a sea of numb
where ships of heart were taken down?
Sunk to the bottom with the one
I hated and I meant to drown.

For in its hull it carried pain
instead of what its purpose was
and thus, I had immense disdain
because it never carried love.

So yes, I set it in my sights
then fired all I had and more.
Carpet-bombing through the night
to sink it to the ocean floor.

And when it finally disappeared,
I flew away and did not know
the other ships were likewise pierced,
doomed just as well to slip below.

They sank at random, one by one.
The ships of pride, and hope, and fear...
of aspiration, sad and fun.
The ship of peace, the ship of tears.

The ship of drive, the ship of will.
No ship was spared the plight went on.
They fell, and fell, and fell, and fell
until at last all ships were gone.

So now in silent flight I go,
no signals come as were before.
No guidance from the sea below.
No hope of landing anymore.

END OF THE LINE

There's a purpose in the way that it goes.
There's a reason why things will be fine.
But we tend to only figure it out...
when we come to the end of the line

PIVOT POINT

He did it because no one else could have done.
Hands raised in praise, yet so few ever know.
I guess it's enough just to know that he won,
but there's more I wanted to understand so

I sought for an answer, unwritten in pen -
why he subjected himself to it all?
Why the injustice from birth until when
the climax when God turned his face to the wall,

leaving him suffering there on his own?
Agony far beyond what man can bare,
purposely facing the cruel cross alone.
A perfect injustice beyond all compare.

Why was this needed? I wondered for years.
Nothing I found helped me understand til,
amidst my search a new question appeared -
what was the void that his grace had to fill?

I'd read that he had to succumb the demands
of justice so that all mankind may be saved,
but who demands justice? I don't understand!"
That's where I was but from there it all changed.

For just like a balance that hangs in the scale,
everything pivots around where it's braced.
So likewise, it all hinges on this detail…
and once I learned it, the rest fell in place.

THIS TIME AROUND

Let it go,
let it flow -
cut it with your words.
Slash at every piece of it
until it finally hurts.

Tear and open up old wounds,
pouring in the salt.
Take aim at it and fire away,
pinning down the fault.

Yeah, all those little thing
that you pathetically hold
onto so desperately
as you continue to get old.

You're like the dog the scripture says -
"to his vomit" it would seem.
Yeah, like a broken record
and you know just what I mean.

But this time you can pack it up
and take all of your shit.
Shove it right straight up your ass!
I am sick of it.

Cuz this time it is different,
I'll no longer be the one
that you can still manipulate.
Baby I am done!

WORLD HISTORY

One struggles beneath the ever-bearing hand of tyranny.
One rises up in revolution, wanting to be free.

One gives his life a soldier so the rest might live in peace.
One celebrates in freedom as they cheer throughout the streets.

One starts his life from nothing but is free to make his way.
One has more than his father at the ending of the day.

One worked for very little yet expected everything.
One sold his vote to get it without ever wondering.

One sat in idle apathy as tyrants raised the hand.
One wonders how it all went wrong... and doesn't understand.

MIDNIGHT

Can you grasp a piece of midnight,
from the furthest reach of the sky,
when it seems nothing has gone right
and there's no reason why?

Can you see yourself from the shadows,
in the place you've been hiding there,
then come to grips with who you are
and finally breathe the air?

For birds believe they're born to fly,
each seed knows it will grow.
So likewise, you'll be who you are…
if at midnight you grasp what you know.

MEMORIES ETCHED

I paused today,
put cares away,
relaxed and let
the moment stay.

Saw feathered skies
through children's eyes,
let time stand still
and realized.

This life of gain
and gathering in,
pursuits of gold,
desires to win.

They offer not
but jaded dust,
doomed to decay
by moth and rust.

And time cares not
nor pardon grants
for foolish charge
or circumstance.

But slowly slips
as grains of sand
through trembling grip
of aging hand.

So, lend an ear
and pause I pray,
take time to let
the moments stay.

For precious times
allowed to be...
etch memories for
eternity.

SINGULARITY

Seconds tick as years go by,
both the same to me.
Time and space be mere illusions…
nothing's as it seems.

Like the wind, we're drifting on
through endless spiral dreams.
Every sense be our delusion…
nothing's as it seems.

As a lad I'd sit and wonder
how it came to be.
Found they keep truth asunder…
nothing's as it seems.

SMILING MIRAGES

The sand of the sea, what are they to me?
Smiling mirages that drift by in lines.
Tried building castles but it seems to be,
the waves take them down every time.

I guess there's a beauty in watching them flow,
like a kaleidoscope, swirling away,
back to their nature where they always go,
leaving me here at the end of the day.

Looking out as the sun sets to the sea,
thinking of what could have been.
Wondering why I'm alone on this shore...
and wishing that I could be them.

COMING TO GRIPS

Sitting here thinking, another week gone.
Another small increment moved from the fire.
It feels like it does when you're just waking up,
half grasping consciousness, half in the mire.

When you're not quite sure if it's real or a dream,
the one where no matter your efforts you fail.
In total frustration you claw just to move,
and in the struggle, you miss the details

that if you had noticed, the dream would be clear.
You'd wake yourself up just to make it all end.
Yet lost in it all the dream goes on and on,
and so the anxiety builds until when

it turns into nightmare, the torment of soul.
You finally wake up in cold beads of sweat.
That's how it feels now that I've come to see
the sum of so many things that I regret.

I'm finally waking up, opening my eyes.
Coming to grips with a life of delusion.
Forced to admit that I've crafted this hell,
here in my tower on the mount of seclusion.

So, I sit here thinking, another week gone.
A glimpse of the fire, miles away so it seems.
Wondering how I'm supposed to go on,
when I can't trust my heart...
and I can't trust my dreams.

TIME

All we have is time
and what comes down the line.
Don't ever think it's more complex than this.

Though the universe - it has no end,
and there is more than one my friend,
too many to be counted. Get the drift?

For we live in eternity,
each day a fiber in a string
that goes on for forever in both ways.

So, use the only thing you have -
your choices, for they forge the path
to how eternally you'll spend your days.

WHAT'S LEFT OF LOVE

Too many nights, too many times
I've woke in sweat and had to find
a way to push you out again,
and pray once more that this will end.

That from my heart you'll finally leave
and not come back into my dreams.

For I am old enough to know
the years have made our love run cold.
And I am wise enough to see…
I only love your memory.

CORIANTUMR AND SHIZ

When your choice is Coriantumr or Shiz,
does it matter what the answer is?

It's kind of like Russian Roulette,
you lose no matter who you get.

To die by fire or die by ice.
Don't really need to think this twice.

We let things slip a bit too far,
now look at what our choices are.

It's sad, but it is what it is -
we're stuck with Coriantumr or Shiz.

GREATNESS

Greatness…

Born of hearts desire,
flame of inner fire.
Dies to quiet fear,
fades and disappears or,

rises like a dove
to the atmosphere above
of contempt and envy
where mediocrity reigns.

For doth not heat rise into the hovering cold
and light disperse into the black of night?
Indeed so.

But greatness finds a way
when guarded day by day.
Encased in iron will,
protected from the chill.
Burning as a glow
for those who find and know
to lock away all aspirations
within the iron vessel of courage.

For heat contained destroys the cold within,
and light encompassed dispels the dark.

Guard therefore
every goal and every dream,
let your purpose go unseen.
Keep it ever tucked away
til at long last come the day
when all shall look
and see...

Greatness.

QUIET EXAMPLE

Tis an interesting thing to consider yet
the value of a quiet example set.

Like the crystal streams, or the mountain air –
consistent, constant, always there.

Blessing every soul who happens by.
Never asking who, never asking why.

Giving joy just by being who they simply are.
Giving light through the night like a brilliant star.

Giving hope to the crowd in the dark abyss.
Yes, it's interesting to consider this.

For life has afforded me such a gift,
a path interwoven with those who lift.

A chance to observe and a chance to learn
what it means to care, what it means to turn

away from the world and it's foolish pride.
Yes, the thought of this makes me look inside

and give thanks to God that I'm in the debt…
of those who a quiet example set.

FROZEN PRIDE

This world of ice.
Forged in frozen sheets,
layer upon layer.
So many attempts to thaw,
daily melting.
Weeping alone, hidden tears
drip from the tips
of every cycle formed.
Crying out, wishing to remain
and finally end the pain,
but it's hard to move
in the cold.

Days are short.
The sun sets
into lonely frost,
silently creeping in.
Progress made to flow
turns again to ice and snow,
leaving nothing to hold
in the chill of this night
but a faint hope
that perhaps tomorrow
I'll find an ounce of courage.

And maybe,
in a silent moment
of light and warmth…
I will turn to you
and finally say,
I'm sorry.

HELL BENT

Running out of time to act,
flashes in the mind.
Running out of everything,
too late to hit rewind.

Wake and take a hammer to it,
crush it to the bone.
Pulverize what's left of it,
make sure all life is gone.

Disregard the letters
in the alphabet arranged,
set to spell the answers out
cuz no one wants the plain.

Go on, drink the poison down.
Taste it coat the tongue.
Pleasure covered minutes
laced to form the web now spun.

Make sure every fool who falls
who couldn't gain control,
stays trapped forever contemplating…
what the demon stole.

THE SMALLEST OF TRIGGERS

I hate how I feel although common it seems,
having been once again what I swore I'd not be.

Yes, despite all the talks that I've had with myself,
making promises to put the past on the shelf.

Asking Heaven to help me and forming a plan,
putting forth my best effort to do all I can.

But so quickly it seems to unravel and fray,
as I learn once again what I learn everyday -

that small problems are made a full universe bigger
if you won't stop what starts... with the smallest of triggers.

DESTINED

Do what you must to ensure they don't see.
Rationalize and pretend it won't be.

Wish it away to escape from it all.
Cover it up like the paint on the wall.

Cloak it in layers of varying hue,
carefully crafted to keep it from view.

Do what you can with all effort and might.
Make every move just to keep it from sight.

Do what you must but in time you will see,
you can't wish away... what is destined to be.

RETURNS

Midst fear and doubt,
when prayers have ceased,
unannounced, without a sound,
returns the clouds
and falls the rain...
again on barren ground.

WHITE ROSE

In a world full of people
so lost in the fight
I've not met another like you,
who midst all the crowd
stands out in the night...
as the white rose of all that is true.

WHAT'S OF THE HEART

What's of the eyes if not to see -
a darkness on the land,
perpetuated by a world
that will not understand.

What's of the ears if not to hear -
a silence through the night.
A deafness born of leaders with
no care of what is right.

What's of the lips if not to speak -
a fading muffled voice,
drowned out by those in power who
refuse the people's choice.

What's of the hands if not to touch -
a plowshare turned to sword,
held high into the east winds where
the dregs of wrath are stored.

What's of the heart if not to feel -
an answer bathed in tears,
that falls as rain on blood-stained soil…
unchanged throughout the years.

SIMPLE WAYS

I woke one day as I recall,
years back in time but not in mind.
The reason I know not at all,
but felt I there and humbled knew,
for peace distilled as morning dew -
life is a gift indeed.

Then from that morn
the years have passed,
whilst way to way filled up the day
and brought me where I stand at last -
worn thin of wear and weak of will.
Yet in my mind the memory still
stirs deep inside my soul.

That life is yet a gift indeed,
with open wings
and wondrous things.
Free to the soul who takes not speed,
but rather stands with thankful heart
and from the simple won't depart
but holds to what is free.

So, now I pause when I awake
with mind that I shall pray and try
to never want nor granted take,
but rather live in simple ways
and cherish what each blessed day...
I'm given holds in store.

IT'S TIME

We want the same and fear the change,
yet all the while we just complain
of everything single thing under the sun.
I've heard it is a general rule,
that man is nothing but a fool
because he never wants the prize he's won.

And yeah, it is the same with me,
I live in discontent you see.
I never seem to find a place to rest.
I've searched to find some middle ground
between the destiny I'm bound
and what I need to change to be my best.

But what I find gets in the way -
that everyone most every day
does not see me the way I see myself.
So, each time that I'm fine with me,
they wish that someone else I'd be.
I end up putting me back the shelf.

But now the time has finally come
where being someone else is done.
It's time to just let go and let it be.
Cuz I can't take another day
of letting things go on this way.
It's time to see what comes...
if I am me.

THE WINDS OF CHANGE

I've never liked the winds of change,
they bring the cold and driving rain.
Destroying what was calm and warm
and leaving nothing but the storm.

They make me have to rise and flee
to higher ground for my safety.
Then when they're done I'm left again
to find new space I can fit in.

And oh the work, it brings me down,
exhausted, humbled to the ground.
Yet in the end, just like before
the calm and sun return once more.

So, I guess should not complain...
but God I hate the winds of change!

THE TRUTH CONCEALED

The deepest hole I've placed it in
and covered it with all that's been.
Then beat upon that grave each day
in hope to make it go away.

I'm terrified that it will grow,
and so afraid somehow, you'll know -
the secret I have buried deep.
The secret that I want to keep.

The thing that is the root of all
the reasons why I want to fall.
The reason why I've never been
able to give love back again.

I know that I should dig it up,
and let you know my feelings but
instead, I'll keep it locked inside…
the truth concealed within my mind.

I USED TO HAVE

I used to have a reason to get up and fight for truth.
I used to have light in my eyes to know I'd be with you.

I used to have a lot of things but now all that I do -
is sit here alone, remembering home, wishing I'd been true.

I used to have a family. I used to have a home.
I used to have friends, things I could call wins,
and a foundation made of stone.

I used to think I'd always haven the things I held on to,
but I lost and they're gone, so I sit here alone…
wishing that I'd been true.

DUSK

When you're on an endless highway, is there any hope at all
that a destination will be reached, and you can finally fall
back in the arms of the one you lost, in the home you left behind?
For despite the years spent traveling, more highway's all I find.

They say that life's a journey, comprised within a dream.
A quest designed to test the will and faith in things unseen.

So, each day when the sun sinks low and the highway fades to dusk,
I look and see you standing there and know I that can trust.
Thus, I keep traveling on and on and fight this empty stare,
and fill the time with dreams of when… I'll finally reach you there.

ETERNAL FIELD

I one time dreamed a dream wherein I walked across an open field,
where every step a memory was, and every breath was poignant
filled.

I saw each day I ever lived, they all bled slowly into one.
Each opportunity to give now stood a moment left undone.

I saw each thing I ever owned and tried so hard to justify,
but every effort woeful fell and I was left to wonder why.

Then as I walked, I looked around in hope to find somewhere to go,
but there was nothing in the field, just sky above and earth below.

Alone was I as time stood still, I shrank within this state of mind.
I felt so infinitely small and realized I had been blind.

For every moment bled together, not a single second gone.
I sought escape and wished to wake but dream and field went on and on.

I walked until I could no more then fell upon my knees to plead,
and in this prayer, I realized how truly desperate was my need.

I spoke a single cry for help and as I did, I woke in sweat.
Then lie there trying to calm myself, still full emerged in self regret.

But finally coming to myself I rose and washed it all away,
resolved to be a better man... and walk with purpose from that day.

THINGS HELD

Holding all
I hold that's mine.
A modern king.
The gifts of time.

Allot no grip,
nor means to hold.
Today in grasp,
yet drifting old.

Begotten days
become as sand.
Slow subtle shift
across barren land.

Things held before
now gone from view.
Fast faded they
like morning dew.

Four seasons passed,
as if a dream.
In winter's chill,
left wondering.

Now looking back
was not as planned,
for in the end…
I naked stand.

SMART PHONES

It's been used in so many movies,
and series, and books to be read -
some kind of sickness breaks out in the world
turning all into the living dead.

I once thought the concept was silly,
but now days I just shake my head.
Because this bug has all the same
turned the whole world…
right into the living dead.

LIGHT THROUGH THE TREES

If you see light through the trees,
don't look away just feel the air.
It brings the whispering on the breeze
so in that moment fix your stare.

For as the tulip breaks through snow
to strive and grow despite the freeze,
the light does likewise pierce below
to find the eye through gaps in leaves.

So in that moment let it be,
and let the full light fill your view.
Then it will be all you can see…
and you will know just what to do.

TIRED EYES

So tired of fighting, don't feel like writing, here in the dark of the night.
As I sit here and sit with my head full of shit that comes pouring
straight out of my life.

Like a weight full of lead, I'd be better off dead,
cuz the cycle would finally end.
No more picking up pieces blown up by releases
and thoughts that I cannot defend.

And I'm tired, oh I'm tired of the way that I'm wired,
and the sad state of what I've become,
that I hide behind smiles,
hand crafted denials built to cover the things that I've done.

But with every day comes a more vast growing sum,
and it fills every night full of dread.
So, I sit here and sit with my head full of shit...
here at the side of my bed.

THE MAN I USED TO BE

Standing at the mirror
someone I no longer know.
Standing there, staring back,
looking all alone.

Says he wants to be like me
but if he only knew,
he'd turn around, walk way,
find something else to do.

For I'm no longer who I was,
the guilt is all on me.
I end up wishing I were him…
the man I used to be.

STAR GAZING

Standing here tonight.
I'm tied to this,
emotionless,
looking at the sky.

A million diamonds shine,
makes me wonder what is mine?
It's been a long, long time
since I saw with open eyes.

Was clear to me back then.
No, I really don't know when,
I fell into the place, hit the race
and started running just to run.

But now I've come to see
you and me
through the eyes that I had then
so, I think the race for us
is done.

For we are not alone.
No, we are not alone.
Take that for what you will,
it is true in every tone.

No, we are not alone.
No, we are not alone.
So take my hand,
let's leave this land...
and we'll finally build our home.

THERE'S LESS THAN TWO HOURS

There's less than two hours
to walk in the sand.
To sail the wide oceans
and see foreign lands.

There's less than two hours
to swing from the stars.
To climb to the top
and look down from afar.

There's so little of time
yet so damn much to see,
and so many things
that I still need to be.

But there's less than two hours,
the clock's running still,
and there's still a dream
that I have to fulfill.

So, let all fade away
til another time when
the two hours are past...
and the dream has been dreamt.

IF ONLY

What are the things that we live for?
Can we honestly say they're the things
that if push came to shove, we would die for?
The thought leaves me contemplating
how totally different it would all be
if for everyone these were the same.
But they're not and I fear someday we'll come to see...
we've only our own selves to blame.

PAGES

Haunted feelings carried by
wings of night as shadows fly.
Drip-drop words from pages then,
feed the fire like oxygen.

Muffled voices through the door.
Phrases I heard long before.
Rhythm opens eyes to see,
lost forgotten parts of me.

Black on white then white again.
Ghostly paths to where I've been.
Keys then press themselves to say -
things I want to hide away.

Trembling hands at last let go.
Breathe again as feeling flow.
Rising vantage rises on.
Poem by poem and song by song
until the dancing leads to lead.
Fast descent, asleep in bed.

Light of dawn at the break of day
melts the night mist fast away.
Then drifting silent to the floor...
are pages as they were before.

LOST

I'm wanting to see just what me I can be.
I'm testing the water to test gravity.

I leap to the sky just to see if I land.
I'm shedding my cover to find where I stand.

I'm spreading my wings cuz I think I can fly.
I pull every trigger and hope I don't die.

I'm loosing my mind just to say that it's lost.
I'm sailing to sea just to see if I'm tossed.

I'm being to be and I'm trying to try.
I do what I do, and I don't question why.

I guess I push limits to find who I am.
I do what I do, and I don't give a damn.

Just where am I going? I never quite know.
I'm just going for going… and it's time to go.

THE ROAD HOME

I stand here on the corner,
steam of breath
rising into the frozen air.
Staring, eyes fixed,
longing to see…
will lights ever emerge
on the horizon of the distant hill?

I've turned asphalt into cobblestone,
coated in black ice
from beat down polished snow.
A work perfected
by so much effort.

So, now I stand and wonder,
who would travel such a road
to where I am?
Who would risk both life and limb?

When you make your path
of isolation sure,
and no one knows what for,
will not all find easier roads
on smooth paved sunlit days?

So, I wait
at this hopeless edge of nowhere
with nothing to do
but struggle against the cold.
Starring up this road
from the most far distant corner...
of the road that leads back home.

THE THIN LINE

A thin line extends to divide faith and fear,
and so often the side you are on isn't clear,
for despite every effort to keep holding on,
and despite every prayer and despite every song
that you've used to inspire and keep faith burning bright,
still the silence creeps in with the still of the night,
and you can't help but wonder, "will it really be fine?"
As the hours roll by... and you walk the thin line.

THOUGHTS FROM THE
BOTTOM OF THE SEA

When I was young, I was eager and free,
believing in something came quite naturally.
Found new things to conquer and new hills to climb,
worked hard for perfection most all of the time.

Dug through information piled high as the sun
to find threads of truth I could weave into one.
I opened my heart and my mind to the sky,
wrapped all things together and understood why.

Dug deep to find purpose and when I was through,
had moments of clarity wherein I knew -
what my life was about, who I am, why I'm here,
then set out to change the world into a sphere.

For I learned how to change the flat plane we are on
into a fine circle of balance and song,
with flowers in the trees bearing fruit on each limb,
a world so much better than what we live in.

So, I worked toward perfection, shaping the plane.
Was told many times that I'm probably insane.
Pulled swords out of stone and defied gravity.
Walked on the water but got lost at sea,

where just like Saint Peter I sank into doubt,
and gasping for air I did not figure out
that the hand of the Lord was extended to save.
So, I sank like a rock to a watery grave.

Now here at the bottom I lie in the cold,
crushed by the weight of a mass overload.
No light can reach me, my striving is through.
No hills to climb and no grand things to do.

No more do I conquer so eager and free.
Pity and doubt are what come naturally,
and the only thing anymore that I perfect...
this long list of everything that I regret.

LESSONS UNLEARNED

The further I go
the worse I get
at what I do
and what I let
destroy my peace
and set me back,
defining well
the things I lack.

You'd think I'd learn.
You'd think I'd see -
the damage done
by being me.
The trail of tears.
The bridges burned.
So many lessons
left unlearned.

STARS ALIGN

So many things we worry of,
so many heartaches find
their way into our lives and hearts
of every single kind.

But it's a fool's game we should know,
for all will be just fine.
We cannot change what's meant to be…
when the stars align.

FROM YESTERDAY

Try on
for trying.
Cry on
for crying.
Die on
for dying.
Fear not to fear.

Hunger's deep
burning.
Awake but
still yearning.
Stones left
o're turning.
Hold to what's dear.

Like the dew
falling.
Faint whisper
calling.
From the ground
crawling.
Be still to hear.

Songs sung
of ages,
break forth
from cages.
Pages on pages.
All becomes clear.

Stand tall
for standing.
All things
demanding.
Grasp
understanding.
Dawn's light is near.

Branches
once traded,
come home
elated.
What was
awaited…
soon will appear.

HOME

Hand on the wheel and mind in the past,
between Lubbock Texas and home..
The sky is as big as the rolling plains vast,
no better place to be alone.

It feels like a movie that's mixed with a dream,
where tranquil and longing roam free.
A place where the ghosts of a thousand years past
still find it their favorite to be.

I can sense them watching from each distant hill,
as I roll through mile after mile.
Again realizing the reason I still...
call Texas my home with a smile.

THE ROOT OF IT ALL

Write me a poem she said from her chair,
and tell the dark secrets that lie under there.

Dig it all up from the deepest of holes.
Tell in your poem what you've not told to a soul.

Write your way through all the layers you've used
to hide the dark secrets that make up the roots
of all of the vines and the thorns in your heart.
Tell me now, what do you hide in the dark?

For you'll never heal if things stay as they are,
with Band-Aids and makeup to cover the scars.

You'll always be there in the state that you're in…
if you won't write it out and let healing begin.

SCULPTURE

Don't try to pour me into a mold.
I'm not made out of plaster...
I'm made out of stone.